Computer Game Developer

Computer Game Developer

Mary Firestone

CHELSEA HOUSE
PUBLISHERS
A Haights Cross Communications Company ®
Philadelphia

CHELSEA HOUSE PUBLISHERS

VP, NEW PRODUCT DEVELOPMENT Sally Cheney
DIRECTOR OF PRODUCTION Kim Shinners
CREATIVE MANAGER Takeshi Takahashi
MANUFACTURING MANAGER Diann Grasse
SERIES DESIGNER Takeshi Takahashi
COVER DESIGNER Takeshi Takahashi

STAFF FOR COMPUTER GAME DEVELOPER

PROJECT MANAGEMENT Ladybug Editorial and Design
DEVELOPMENT EDITOR Tara Koellhoffer
LAYOUT Gary Koellhoffer

A Haights Cross Communications ✦ Company ®

www.chelseahouse.com

First Printing

9 8 7 6 5 4 3 2 1

Library of Congress Cataloging-in-Publication Data

Firestone, Mary.
   Computer game developer / Mary Firestone.
      p. cm. — (Weird careers in science)
   Includes bibliographical references and index.
   ISBN 0-7910-8700-X
   1. Computer games—Programming. I. Title. II. Series.
   QA76.76.C672F585 2005
   794.8'1526—dc22

                                    2005012074

006.696

FIR

CAREERS

TABLE OF CONTENTS

1

Introduction

WICKED2 TWINS HAVE INVADED the island home of Crash Bandicoot, revealing their plans to enslave Crash and his friends and devastate their world. To face this great evil, Crash must team up with his creator and archenemy, Dr. Cortex. Also along for the adventure are Dr. Cortex's young niece, Nina, and Crash's sister, Coco. Who are the Twins? They want revenge against Dr. Cortex, but why? And where are they from?

Computer game designers spend hours creating stories like this one, inventing enemies, challenges, and new environments for characters like Crash Bandicoot. Their career passions were developed during their childhood and teen years, when they played computer games for hours, sometimes even for days, on end. As adults and design professionals, they rarely grow tired of playing games or coming up with ideas for new games. A love of games is fundamental to being a successful computer game designer.

If you're into gaming, your parents may show concern as you spend hours trying to get to the next level of a challenging game (Figure 1.1). However, studies now show that computer game players make better drivers, soldiers, and surgeons, because their reaction time (improved by all that wrist-twisting practice with the game controller) is faster and they have better peripheral (side) vision. Game-playing involves taking risks, and the worlds within computer games present many challenges that require the player to pay attention on many levels at once. In a story for *careers.com*, Daniel Rubin wrote, "researchers at New York's Beth Israel Medical Center found that doctors who spent at least three hours a week playing video games made fewer mistakes, and performed laparoscopic surgery [surgery done with the aid of a lighted tube] faster than their non-playing peers."

A typical day for a computer game designer varies. Depending on the designer's area of expertise, he or she might spend the day programming software, creating storylines, or creating three-dimensional (3D) animation. Or the designer might be brainstorming ideas with fellow team members to try to decide which moves a character should make next.

Lead designers leave it to their teams to work out any potential problems in a game, such as gridlocks (when the game freezes). Game designers often have to work out problems or "**bugs**" (when a game functions improperly

Figure 1.1 This young man is playing Sonic the Hedgehog. Some studies show that computer games improve reaction time and peripheral vision.

due to mistakes in software) in a game at the last minute, so they work long hours under tremendous pressure. A single video game can take years to develop.

Large companies such as Activision, Nintendo, Atari, and Sega have been hiring video game designers for over 30 years. Today, there are hundreds of game development companies and corporations, both small and large, that employ game designers of all kinds. Talented designers sometimes hire their own teams and start a new company. The options for game designers today are growing fast. In fact, the sky's the limit.

2

The History of Computer Game Design

MANY EXPERTS IN THE GAMING business trace the roots of computer games back to the pinball machines of the 1920s (Figure 2.1), or even further, to the late 1800s and a game called Bagatelle, which was a type of billiard game. Both games used a slanted board, with balls that fell into cups for points.

In 1931, gaming enthusiast and inventor David Gottlieb created a game called Baffle Ball, which used a plunger to launch balls up a slope, an improvement on the simpler games of the day. Around this time, advances in electrical circuit design made it possible for an electronics whiz named Harry Williams to invent Contact, the first electric pinball machine, in 1933.

Figure 2.1 Pinball machines first became popular in the 1920s.

These board and pinball games were set up in Penny Arcades, along boardwalks at seaside resorts, and at amusement parks and state fairs around the country.

THE FIRST COMPUTER GAME

In the 1950s and 1960s, computers existed, but they were gigantic—big enough to fill whole rooms (Figure 2.2). Before the invention of the **silicon microchip**, all the electronic connections in computers were made with large **transistors** and glass **vacuum tubes**. These parts got extremely hot when the computers were running, so the machines had to have cooling systems inside them to keep them from starting fires. The cooling systems, along with the hundreds of components, took up a lot of space. The information early computers generated wasn't stored on disks, but on punchcards and ticker tape, which took up even more room. Still, engineers and designers didn't let the awkwardly huge sizes bother them. They kept tinkering, trying to make computer games.

WILLIAM HIGINBOTHAM AND TENNIS FOR TWO

Many game enthusiasts consider William A. Higinbotham, a fun-loving physicist, the true inventor of computer games. Higinbotham loved pinball. As an employee of Brookhaven National Laboratory (BNL), a government center for scientific research, it seemed unlikely that he would be able to bring that interest into his work. But that is exactly what he did, starting a powerful trend that mixes fun and engineering.

Figure 2.2 The UNIVAC, one of the first computers, was so large it took up an entire room.

In 1958, Higinbotham used his technical know-how to create a game he called Tennis for Two, as an attraction for BNL's Visitors Day. Higinbotham said he created the game because he wanted to "liven up the place" with a game, "which could convey the message that our scientific endeavors have relevance to society."

Higinbotham's Tennis for Two was displayed on an **oscilloscope** with a small (5 inches in diameter) round screen. The electronics that ran it were large vacuum tubes, relays, and transistors. When it was all put together, it was the size of a couple of refrigerators.

According to records at Brookhaven Laboratory, Tennis for Two "turned out to be a real crowd pleaser." The screen was later enlarged from 5 inches to 15 inches in diameter, and players could choose to play "low-gravity tennis" on the moon, or "high-gravity tennis" on Jupiter. The system took Higinbotham about two hours to design, and "a couple of days to fill it in with the components," according to "The First Video Game," a story about Higinbotham on Brookhaven's Website.

STEVE RUSSELL AND SPACE WARS

Steve Russell, a pioneer in computer game development, created a game called Space Wars, which used a large computer. He began the project while he was a student at Massachusetts Institute of Technology (MIT) and was part of a group called the Tech Model Railroad Club (TMRC). The group encouraged creative engineering among its members, and enjoyed building systems, of all kinds just to "see how things worked."

Space Wars involved two spaceships (the *Wedge* and the *Needle*) in battle. Players could choose their speed and direction, and control their torpedo firings. Russell said, "The spaceship controls were four switches. One [switch] let you rotate counterclockwise, another was for rotating clockwise, one fired your rocket for thrust, and the last one fired your torpedoes," according to *The Ultimate History of Video Games*.

Members of the TMRC made some changes to Space Wars, adding stars for the background and a sun. Space Wars ran on a computer system the size of a refrigerator and cost $120,000. It laid the foundation for later computer and video game systems. Because of its size and expense, it was never sold on the open market.

RALPH BAER: THE FATHER OF VIDEO GAMES

Another early inventor of computer games was Ralph Baer, who is sometimes called the "Father of Video Games." He created the first home video game system, Odyssey, which was later produced by Magnavox, the television manufacturer.

Bill Gates

After inventing Space Wars, Steve Russell left MIT and moved to Seattle, Washington, to take a job at a computer company. The engineers and designers at his company tested their newly designed computers' resistance to "crashing" by bringing in kids from local schools and letting them bang away on the keyboards. Bill Gates was one of those kids. According to Russell, Gates "was the only kid who could crash them no matter what."

Baer began his career in computer game design when he was asked to create computer simulations of military encounters, to help train soldiers in the U.S. military. He called his design the "TV Game." It consisted of different types of chase games, and had a "light gun" for shooting. In 1968, Baer filed for a **patent**, and continued to develop computer games, including ping-pong, volleyball, handball, and hockey.

NOLAN BUSHNELL: FATHER OF THE INDUSTRY

Around the same time, an inventor named Nolan Bushnell became obsessed with Steve Russell's Space Wars, while he was an engineering student at the University of Utah. He loved Space Wars so much, he memorized all of its moves, playing it late into the night.

After leaving college, Bushnell went to work for Ampex Corporation in Redwood City, California, as an engineer. During his free time, he built computer games with the company's spare parts. He eventually created a game called Computer Space, using an old black-and-white television he got from Goodwill as the monitor. He found a company to produce his game, but it turned out to be too complicated for the average player and didn't sell well.

Bushnell moved on and started his own company, naming it Atari, after the Japanese word for "check," as in the game of chess. Because of his important contributions to the computer game industry, he would become known as the Father of the Industry (Figure 2.3).

Pong

After Atari was up and running, Nolan Bushnell hired someone to design a game based on ping-pong. The first

Figure 2.3 Nolan Bushnell, sometimes called the "Father of the (video game) Industry," later became famous for starting the chain of Chuck E. Cheese restaurants, which combined food and video games in one location.

Pong machine, as it came to be known, was placed in a tavern called Andy Capp's in Sunnyvale, California. This first version of the game attracted so many players, it broke down, as the story goes, from an overflowing coin box.

Atari was able to expand with the financial success of Pong. It went on to create other games, including Gotcha, which was a maze game; Trak 10, the first racing game; and another racing game, called Grantrak 10. Other early Atari games included Space Race, Steeple Chase, Stunt Cycle, and Maneater. These games were available in home video consoles and arcade versions. The Atari 2600 was the most popular video console game system in 1977.

VIDEO CARTRIDGES IMPROVE GAMES
BUT HURT THE INDUSTRY

With the invention of the microprocessor, Fairchild Camera and Instrument produced a system in 1976 that would let players switch games by inserting different game cartridges. All previous computer game systems had been designed to run only one game. The following year, Atari designed a system called the VCS (video computer system) 2600. It came with nine games, all on different cartridges. The VCS also had a **joystick** and switches for selecting levels of difficulty. Other companies began to design systems that could do the same thing. However, nothing could revive the novelty of video games, which had worn off, and the market crashed. Large manufacturers of games, such as

Microprocessors

A microprocessor (also called a microchip, or chip) is a small, thin, black rectangular unit with circuits inside it. It is the central processing unit and heart (and brain) of any computer, including video game consoles. It is where the instructions are stored for carrying out software applications, such as video games. Microprocessors replaced larger central processing units, since they were more convenient, with their miniaturized electronic components. Over the years, game systems increased the number of bits in their microprocessors, starting with 8-bit systems, then 16-bit systems, and eventually 32- and 64-bit systems, up to the current powerful 128-bit system of today, called the "Emotion Engine" of the Sony Playstation2. Each increase in bytes increases a system's computing power.

Magnavox and Atari, sold their remaining games at reduced rates.

PAC-MAN AND THE REVIVAL OF THE VIDEO GAME FIELD

The market for video games remained in a slump until Pac-Man arrived on the shores of the United States from Japan. It quickly became the next big thing in arcades. Designed in 1980 for Ramco, a Japanese gaming company, by a pinball wizard named Toru Iwatani, it was the first computer arcade game that appealed to both women and men (Figure 2.4). Iwatani made sure that Pac-Man was not only nonviolent, but looked happy and cute. It was available on home game consoles, such as Atari 2600, Commodore, and Intellivision.

The game was originally named "Puckman" (from the Japanese term *paku paku*, which refers to the motion of the mouth opening and closing while eating). Pac-Man was the first video game to introduce a specific character, the little round dot-eater. Pac-Man, a round shape with a chomping mouth, "ate" his way through rows and rows of dots, which were lined up in a maze pattern. At the same time, Pac-Man was chased by four ghosts, or monsters, who wandered through the maze, trying to catch and eat him. Four dots, called power-pills, or energizers, provided Pac-Man with extra energy, so that he could eat the monsters (instead of being eaten *by* them) when they got too close. When Pac-Man ate a power-pill, the monsters turned blue and ran away from him.

Every dot Pac-Man ate was worth 10 points, and power pills were worth 50. Pac-Man gained even more points if he ate fruits. For cherries, he got 100 points each; strawberries

Figure 2.4 Computer game developer Massaya Nakamura plays the arcade version of Pac-Man.

were worth 300 points. The highest points were awarded for eating a bell, a key, or the Yellow Enemy from Galaxian, which gained Pac-Man a whopping 2,000 points.

Monsters in the game had different colors, names, nicknames, and unique personal traits: Shadow (Blinky) was red, Speedy (Pinky) was pink, Bashful (Inky) was light blue, and Pokey (Clyde) was orange.

Because of Pac-Man's success, the video game business shifted away from racing and shooting games. Game manufacturers turned their efforts to Pac-Man–like maze chases, with animals. Some examples are Mappyland with mice, Pengo with penguins, and Congo Bongo with monkeys. The success of these games created a "boom" in the arcade business. Suddenly, video arcades were being installed in hotel lobbies, grocery stores, and community centers. In a study from 1982, researchers found that there were 1.5 million arcade games in the United States.

NEW COMPANIES AND GAMES

In 1980, Nintendo, another Japanese company, introduced the game Donkey Kong to arcades. Donkey Kong was given its name by its Japanese designer, Shigeru Miyamoto, who wanted to find the best American terms for a stubborn gorilla. He chose the word *donkey* for the animal's stubborn qualities, and *kong*, after the giant gorilla from monster films like *King Kong*. The game was revolutionary for its time, featuring colorful characters and distinct levels of play.

Nintendo created many variations of Donkey Kong and its main character, Mario. Some of these included Super Mario Brothers, Super Mario Brothers 3, Super Mario 64, and Donkey Kong Country.

Naming Mario

Mario (of Mario Brothers and Donkey Kong fame), was named after Mario Segale, the landlord who owned Nintendo's warehouse. Minoru Arakawa, the manager for Nintendo operations in the United States, hadn't been able to pay the warehouse rent because of slow sales. Mario Segale, the landlord, was upset and had an argument with Arakawa. Segale finally agreed to wait for the rent payment. After that, Arakawa changed the original name of the Donkey Kong character, "Jumpman," to "Mario," in the landlord's honor.

As microchip technology improved, Sony entered the scene as a manufacturer of video game systems, introducing the Playstation game console in 1994, joining Sega, Atari, and Nintendo in the home video game console business. Large video game publishers such as Nintendo, Activision, and Electronics Arts, Inc., now compete in this multibillion-dollar industry. Microsoft XBOX, Sony PlayStation2, and Nintendo Gamecube are the main competitors in the game system market.

Chapter 3

Types of Computer Games

THE PLATFORM GAME

PLATFORM GAMES BEGAN with Donkey Kong. In a platform game, the player advances by making the characters jump from one platform to the next, gaining power and points as they fight enemies.

ADVENTURE GAMES

Most computer games are adventure games. They involve exploration, puzzle-solving, and interaction between game characters. Escape From Monkey Island (LucasWare) and Syberia (Dreamcatcher Interactive) are two such games.

EDUCATIONAL GAMES

Educational games are designed to teach people, usually children, about a certain subject, or to help them learn a skill as they play.

FIGHTING GAMES

Fighting games have characters in a fight, usually involving martial arts. These games are usually found in arcades with **fixed shooters** (Figure 3.1). Some examples of fixed shooter fighting games are XPilot, Freedom Fighters, and Space War.

Figure 3.1 This young man is using a fixed shooter to play Silent Scope in a video arcade.

FIRST-PERSON SHOOTER

A first-person shooter (FPS) is a computer or video game where the view of the game world simulates the main character's view. Flight simulators are examples of first-person shooter games.

THIRD-PERSON SHOOTER

A third-person shooter is a computer game in three dimensions. The camera view is outside and usually behind the main player character. Star Trek: Deep Space Nine is a third-person shooter game.

MASSIVE MULTIPLAYER ONLINE GAMES

A massive multiplayer online game (MMOG) is a type of computer game where hundreds or thousands of players play all at once against and with each other in a game world to which they are all connected via the Internet.

Sony released its first MMOG, PlanetSide, in the spring of 2003. PlanetSide is a first-person shooter game, set in a futuristic world called Auraxis. Three warring factions—the Terran Republic, the Vanu Sovereignty, and the New Conglomerate—are battling for control of Auraxis and its ancient alien artifacts. Players can join any of the three factions and fight on foot, from vehicles, in the air, or from places that hold a variety of guns and equipment.

MUSIC

A music video game is also known as a rhythm game. It focuses entirely around the player's ability to follow a musical beat and stay with the rhythm of the game's soundtrack. Music games in arcades have lighted dance floors, and the player has to follow a set of cues (Figure 3.2). In

Figure 3.2 Dancing games like this one, Dance Dance Revolution, test the rhythm of the players.

most music video games, the player must press specific buttons in time with the game's music.

PUZZLE GAMES

Computer puzzle games are about puzzle-solving. Different types of puzzles involve logic, strategy, pattern recognition, sequences, word completion, or, in some cases, just pure luck. Tetris is an example of a popular puzzle game.

RACING

Racing games exist for both video and computers. Players sometimes use a "steering wheel" device, which simulates an actual driving experience on screen.

ROLE-PLAYING VIDEO GAME

Role-playing video games, or RPGs, as gamers call them, involve intricate plots and character development. Players advance through a large number of vehicles, weapons, and abilities. They must choose from several combinations of skills for their character, based on what they think will help them advance or win the game.

Game developers from Blizzard Entertainment have designed a role-playing game called World of Warcraft. As a massive multiplayer game, this RPG gives thousands of players expansive 3D environments to choose from, including mountains, deserts, and forests. Players can choose the role or character they want to be. They can be a human, a night elf, an orc, a tauren, or a dwarf in a variety of game challenges.

SERIOUS GAMES

Serious games (SGs) are a category of video and computer games that do not have entertainment as their primary aim. Instead, a serious game is usually a simulation that has the look and feel of a game, but is actually a simulation of real-world events or processes. The main goal of a serious game is usually to train or educate users (though it may have other purposes, such as marketing) while giving them an enjoyable experience. The fact that serious games are meant to be at least somewhat entertaining encourages people to use them over and over again. Although the U.S. government and medical professionals are the largest users of serious games (Figure 3.3), other sectors of business and commerce are beginning to see the benefits of such simulations and are actively seeking to develop these kinds of tools.

Figure 3.3 The U.S. Army uses serious games to help train soldiers for combat.

SHOOT 'EM UP

A shoot 'em up ("shmup" for short) is a video game in which the player has limited control over his or her character. The focus is almost entirely on trying to kill or defeat the character's enemies. Serious Sam is a type of shoot 'em up game.

SIMULATION

A simulation game (also known as a game of status or mixed game) is a mixture of a game of skill, a game of chance, and a game of strategy. This combination results in a simulation of a complex structure (like a stock exchange or changing civilization). The Sims became the most popular game of this type.

SPORTS

Sports games can be either computer or video games that simulate the playing of traditional sports. Football: Madden NFL, Golf: Tiger Woods PGA Tour, Wakeboarding: Wakeboarding Unleashed, and Basketball: NBA Live are some of the most popular sports games.

STRATEGY

In strategy games, the players' skill typically determines the outcome. Most computer and video games include some element of strategy. Strategy involves looking ahead, imagining and mentally planning outcomes to eliminate or defeat an opponent. Two strategy games for the PC (personal computer) are Yugi-oh Online and Tin Soldiers: Julius Caesar.

The Sims

The Sims is a game where virtual people called Sims are placed under the control of the player in a virtual "dollhouse." The player controls their daily activities such as sleeping, eating, cooking, and bathing. The objective of the game is to organize the Sims' time to help them achieve personal goals.

Sims characters have some amount of free will. So, even if you tell them to do something, they might do something else first, or even ignore you completely.

Daily maintenance requirements must also be scheduled, such as personal hygiene, meals, and sleep. If the simulated people do not get the right amount of maintenance, they get sick and die. Financial health is simulated by having the Sims find jobs, go to work, pay bills, and take advantage of social contacts to advance in their jobs.

Chapter 4

Computer Game Designers

MORE THAN MOST CAREERS, the working life of a computer game designer combines work and play. Today, more than ever, designing games is mostly about hard work, because the industry is expanding and has become extremely competitive. A successful computer game can earn a company millions of dollars in profits. Game publishers and studios are constantly competing intensely for the biggest piece of the gaming action.

WHAT DOES A COMPUTER GAME DESIGNER DO?

Computer game designers have a unique combination of artistic talent and engineering skills. They must also have good

interpersonal skills, because games are created through teamwork. A video game designer might be a producer, an audio engineer, a computer software engineer, a cinematographer, a writer, a director, or an artist.

The technical description of the job goes something like this: Computer game designers create games for home video and handheld game systems, computers, and arcades. They work in **studios**, in four distinct areas: design, artistic, programming, and testing.

Computer game developers work for large publishers, such as Activision, Nintendo, THQ, Electronic Arts Inc., and Ubi Soft, which market and distribute the games to **retailers** around the world. Studios are smaller operations, compared to the publishers that own them.

HOW GAMES ARE DESIGNED

Computer game design is an exciting field, because it takes advantage of computer technology, which is always getting better. Designers apply these improvements in sound and visuals to games, to make them more colorful, interesting, and interactive.

The stages of computer game development include:

- coming up with an idea
- creating **storyboards**
- creating a **design document**
- creating the game
- **debugging** the game.

These phases are accomplished by development teams that fall into a few basic categories: designers, artist-animators, game programmers, and testers.

KINDS OF DESIGNERS
Lead Designers

Lead designers start things off by getting their team members together and engaging them in creative brainstorming sessions. If they're designing a game for a movie theme, such as *Spider-Man*, the main character is the focus, but they still have to dream up his physical world; where objects and buildings go; other characters in the story, including helpers and enemies; and power sources. This all begins in sessions where ideas are tossed around, laughed at, seriously explored, or rejected entirely. Storyboards are created from these brainstorming sessions, and are posted on a wall in rows, so that the group can work with the events of a game more easily. Storyboards have rough sketches of characters and contain short scripts that describe the action or dialogue.

Lead designers decide on the overall concept for the game. They do not have the last word, however; executives at high levels of the company must also give their approval. Once everyone accepts the idea for the game, lead designers decide on the game's **mission, theme** (the overall idea), and rules.

Lead designers are also responsible for the overall tone (whether it is silly, intense, mysterious, or playful) and quality of a game, setting its mood. Sometimes, they play the role of **producer** or **lead programmer** as well. Regardless of their official job description, they are always the leaders of the process. If some aspect of the game isn't working with the overall theme, the lead designer's job is to get rid of it. Lead designers always have to keep their minds focused on the overall picture and scope of the game.

Lead designers try to form a strong idea of what the character's personality is like, what his or her skills are, and how he or she will fulfill the goals of the game. They ask themselves: What does the character look like? What are his special talents? Is he able to fly? Who are his enemies? What are his unique personality traits? Is he funny? Clever? Wily? How does he lose his energy, and how can he regain it? Who are the other characters in the game? How do they help fulfill the mission or goal of the game?

Lead designers must have good people skills and management skills. They must know how to handle the **budget** for creating the game and keep team members on schedule. Technical expertise is also important for a lead designer, because he or she needs to be able to communicate with programmers about bugs in the game, or anything that isn't working and why it isn't working. Often, lead designers get their jobs after spending many years in the field as programmers, level designers, producers, or testers.

Level Designers

After the concept for the game has been agreed upon by team members, **level designers** go to work to create different challenges for players. Just about all video games can eventually be won. Players defeat a game by meeting the challenges of several levels of difficulty. Each level has a unique environment and set of skills for the characters. When players meet the challenges, they advance to the next level. Level designers work with programmers and artistic teams to help create interesting distinctions between levels. The trick for level designers is to come up with challenges that aren't too hard, but also aren't too easy. If level challenges frustrate the player too much with their difficulty, players won't want to try to get to the next level. If a level is too easy, players will get bored. Boredom must be avoided at all costs. One level may leave a player with a racing heart, but if the next level isn't up to the player's ability, he or she will stop playing. Level designers always have to ask themselves, "Is this game fun?" They need to be completely honest with themselves about the answer if they want to produce the best game possible.

Another way level designers stay on top of their game is by playing the games made by their competitors. If they can outpace the competition with their own brand of fun, chances are their games will win the hearts and minds of new players.

Artist-Animators

What would make you want to play a game over and over again? Level challenges and dramatic storylines might keep you interested for a while, but in the end, it will take more than that. The right combination of story and challenge must be mixed with eye-grabbing, colorful visuals to make a good game a *great* game.

This is the job of the video game artist. Computer game artists do whatever they can to hold the player's attention. They work with lead designers during the **concept** development phase, creating illustrations from sketches, and enhancing it with colors and images that add interest or help tell the story (Figure 4.1).

Video and computer games are created in two dimensions, three dimensions, or a combination of both. Two-dimension (2D) artists make tiles, textures, and "**skins**" for games. They often create sketches during the early stages of the design. Three-dimension (3D) artists make models that fit the theme of the game. Models may be of people,

Figure 4.1 Game designers use their computers to add color, characters, and interesting backgrounds to their games.

cars, or buildings. Both create images inside a computer. 2D artists often scan photographs into the computer as surface textures.

There are four kinds of 3D artists who work on a game: character artists, animators, background designers, and texture artists.

Character Artists

Character artists begin by sketching out an image on paper—something that looks like the character the lead designer had in mind. He or she spends a lot of time studying the concept for the game to try to understand the goal of the game, making sure the character's movement and appearance fit in with the theme. How much damage can a character deliver in a confrontation? What are its weapons? How does the character get back its health after a battle? These are some questions character artists keep in mind as they come up with designs. After the artists complete the design on page, they go to their computers and begin to build it with modeling software, starting with shapes called **polygons**.

All objects in a game start out as polygons. They are then layered with textures that help identify the object as what it is supposed to represent. In other words, a cement wall may begin as a four-sided polygon, and later, it is given a cement-like surface to make it look real. When designers build characters this way, the software in the computer acts like a sculpting tool. The shape can be twisted and moved in any direction, as if it were in the artists' hands.

Animators

Animators are responsible for getting the characters to move around the game in a realistic way. They work with a script and create movements needed for the specific story or action. To develop an action sequence, the artist sets the character in motion by choosing moves and entering them on the keyboard. The computer makes the

Polygons

The word *polygon* comes from two Greek words: *poly*, which means "many," and *gonos*, which means "angle." A polygon is any closed path made up of straight lines. The straight lines are called sides or edges, and the points where the sides meet are the polygon's vertices. If a polygon is simple, then its sides (and vertices) create the boundary of the polygon's region.

movements look realistic according to preset formulas in the software.

Animators study the anatomy of both humans and animals to get a better understanding of muscular and skeletal structures, and the ways real creatures move in the natural world. Realism is important to the overall feeling of the game, so animators must understand these bodily structures well.

If a character is experiencing a feeling, it has to be synchronized (fit in; match) with an action in the game. Animators work from a script, to match a character's expression of feeling with the appropriate game actions. Animators also add facial expressions and body language to give characters unique personalities. A character's emotional reaction helps the animator decide on a certain movement, as well as the tone. Animators create two kinds of action sequences: **cut scenes**, which are short movies that play during the game, and **player-controlled action**, like running, jumping, and talking.

Another way to create realistic action in a game is to use real-world elements. A technique called **motion capture** involves using real actors with **sensors** attached to their bodies. Computers record the actors' movements. Later, the artists fill in the textures and shading to complete the animation.

Animators must have a good combination of basic art skills and technical skills. They must be able to build real structures from clay, and then photograph and scan them into a computer, where they can be animated later by character artists using modeling software.

Background Designers

In the video game version of *Spider-Man*, the main character swings freely between the darkened alleys of New York

City. The horizon is a dramatic blue-black, and a yellow glow of city life and traffic buzzes far below on the street. This scene—the city and its twilight setting—is all the creation of background artists. They produce the environments in which the characters act out their action sequences or level challenges. These environments, or backgrounds, can be massive crowd scenes at a football stadium or baseball park, or the amusement park atmosphere of Mario Party 6.

Background art, put simply, is anything that doesn't move in a game scene. Background artists make sketches based on what they've seen in the original design concept. They must pay close attention to scale, which tells them whether the size of characters fits in with the background scenery. They use modeling software to fill out the environment, according to the role of the objects in the game.

With two-dimensional games, backgrounds are created with pen and paper, then scanned into the computer. Background artists fill in the background with **paint programs,** such as Paint Shop Pro or Adobe Photoshop.

Texture Artists

Texture artists use computer software to create surface textures such as skin, hair, and clothing. Texture artists work with photographs or create the surface image themselves by painting a picture to achieve the precise effect they want. A tiger's fur or the rough metal of a shield being used in battle is produced by a texture artist. After texture artists achieve the look they want, they photograph it or simply scan the image into a computer. When the image appears on the computer, they place it around the object's polygon, "wrapping" the image around an object. This process is called **texture mapping**.

Programmers

Games are set up so that players have a sense of being the main character in the game. This can be done by switching points of view or just from having the controller in the player's hand, animating the action in the game. All of these actions are created first by the designer and written out in the design document. Programmers take this information and write software code that fulfills the game goals.

Programmers must be able to project how much time it will take to write code for a particular application in the game. Design schedules are strict and deadlines are not easily changed. Programmers usually work in groups. Each takes on the work for a particular section of the game. The programmers plan the code, by creating their own **algorithms**. The programming languages used most often in game development are **C**, **C++**, and **Java**.

Programmers who work in game development are responsible for how well the game runs. The program tells the computer or video game system what to do with the information it is being given. Programmers are allowed to express their creativity by writing code that enhances or deepens the player's experience.

Sound Designers

Sound designers help create the mood of a game. They produce the sounds of massive bomb explosions, car crashes, the zing of disappearing enemies, and twinkling clouds of fairy dust.

Music plays an important role in the atmosphere of a video game. If music increases in its volume, or changes from a delicate, sparkling quality to a dark and foreboding one, players pay attention. Sound is used to produce a sense of something to come, but it should never become the central focus of a game. If the music doesn't match the tone of the game, players will notice and perhaps not want to play anymore.

Sound designers have a strong background in music composition, and know about all musical instruments. They can create the sound of a full orchestra with computers, which have digitally stored sound **bytes** that sound like the real thing. They can create a string quartet or a rock band playing a tune with a driving beat. Sound designers sometimes work in sound studios, so they have to understand the techniques of a recording. Sound designers usually have experience with **digital** and **analog** recording techniques.

Chapter 5

Tools of the Computer Game Designer

IN THE EARLY DAYS of animation, artists drew each frame of action, changing each frame slightly, to create the illusion of movement. These drawings were photographed in a series called **animatics**, and sent out to **cinematographers** who made them into live-action films. In these old cartoons, the characters looked like they were actually moving. Traditional animation is still done, but today, most cartoons and video games are created within a computer, as whole creatures. They are animated not by a flurry of slightly changing photos of drawings, but with software that understands what it is trying to do, and then actually moves the character according to its preset goals and tasks.

41

With computer technology, video game designers can invent whole worlds and missions, with increasingly complex levels and demands on players' skills of observation and attention. To do this, they use the high-tech tools of computer software and scanning equipment, along with low-tech tools like storyboards, design documents, and drawing materials.

STORYBOARDS

The storyboard is the first tool of game development. After the initial phase of brainstorming, designers sketch out the plot. The storyboard may include an actual plot, or it may be a series of worlds that the character enters and leaves as the player advances through each level of the game.

Storyboards are like a map, which designers create as they picture how a game will look when it is finished. It often consists of several main ideas:

- a sketch of the character
- a description of the action
- notes about sounds and dialogue
- technical notes and instructions.

Goal Accomplished

Virtually all video games are produced with some sort of goal for the player to achieve (Figure 5.1). In Super Mario 64, Mario's goal is to rescue a princess. In SuperSmash Bros. Melee, a 2001 release, a variety of characters take on challenges, and players can choose from 20 different stages of battle as they make their way through each level. The only goal is to "defeat" the game with the weapons available.

Storyboards are placed in order according to the sequence of events. The nice thing about having the game on boards, or cards, is that designers can shuffle them around as they make changes in the way game events take place.

Each individual storyboard is called a **frame**, and the frames usually represent the different levels of the game.

Designers look at the storyboards to figure out the rules and structure of the game. For example, if Mario encounters Donkey Kong on the first level, he struggles hard to defeat him, and loses. However, if he can get to the gold coins dotted overhead on his path, he has a chance to beat Donkey Kong. So, Mario has to avoid Donkey Kong until he has enough energy to defeat him. When Mario does this, he gets another dose of energy, which allows him to overcome more difficult challenges.

Figure 5.1 Game designer Shigeru Miyamoto demonstrates his Super Mario game.

Designers map out different worlds. They place buildings, platforms, trees, and caves in strategic ways to create the atmosphere intended by the storyline and lead designer.

DESIGN DOCUMENTS

The design document contains all the information that members of the team will need: the overall story of the game, the characters and environments, levels, and instructions on who is responsible for which area of the design (such as sound, dialogue, and graphics). The design document is where team members record what occurs as the game is developed. Design documents contain everything a player might encounter during play—all the sights, sounds, characters, and challenges.

COMPUTER SOFTWARE

After the storyboards and design documents are created, the programmers go to work on creating code in C, C++, or Java, computer languages that tell the computer how to generate frameworks of objects. Programmers also use software from other projects. Studios store software from previous games, and programmers draw on existing games as needed. They generate some of the modeling software, or the "**3D engine**," for creating polygons with all the right shadows and textures for the surfaces of objects. Some art and modeling programs include 3D Studio Max, Maya, Lightwave, and SoftImage.

Artificial intelligence is another kind of software application that game designers use. It controls the movement of objects and detects interactions and collisions.

When the objects are created according to the design document guidelines, they are entered into something called a **tool chain**, which combines the computer codes into one large unit, or piece of code. *Tool chain* is a software designer's term. It refers to a series of processes used for programming computer software, which makes the game work in the desired way.

CINEMATOGRAPHY

Cinematography is the art and science of photography in making films. Computer game designers occasionally use film in their production of games, to create an effect. Within the game itself, players can interact with the film characters, or take part in the movie-like atmosphere created by special camera techniques. These techniques involve the placement of "cameras" at certain angles, for example, to focus on one character's actions instead of another.

HANDHELD SYSTEMS

The race for the newest, best technology in the video game business is going strong, especially for handheld systems. The leap from the much simpler one-player technology to wireless multiplayer games has been made by two major players in the industry, currently going head-to-head in the handheld marketplace: Sony, with PlayStation Portable (PSP) and Nintendo DS Console.

A Brief History of the Handheld System

The handheld system, or console, is great for its convenience: It combines the screen, the system software and controls in one unit small enough to pop in your backpack, purse, or even the side pocket of your favorite pair of pants. At first, the convenience of handheld systems made them appealing, but players soon discovered that these systems had their share of problems.

One of the most popular of these early handheld systems

was Microvision, released by Milton Bradley in 1979. It was designed by an engineer named Jay Smith, who later went on to design a very popular system called Vectrex, an arcade-like tabletop game system.

Microvision's innovation was its combination of single game cartridges and **portability**. But its limited number of games, small screen, and no backup system caused its failure in the marketplace. Production of Microvision systems ended in 1981. Other companies tried making handheld systems, such as Game Gear by Sega, TurboExpress by NEC, and Supervision, to name a few.

In 1989, Nintendo released Game Boy, the best-selling handheld game system to date. The first Game Boy had a tiny black and green **LCD** screen, an eight-way directional pad, and two action buttons. Game Boy games came in small detachable cartridges. Tetris was the game most often played on Game Boy, and is considered responsible for Game Boy's enormous early success. Tetris was originally a computer game designed by Russian inventor Alexey Pajitnov in 1985. It is one of the best-known computer games ever made, thanks partly to its success as a Game Boy game. It has been designed for nearly every game machine available.

Game Boy didn't change much until 1998, when Nintendo released Game Boy Color, an improvement over the black and green screens of the past. Game Boy Advance came next, in 2001. It had extra buttons, a larger screen, and greater computing power. Other companies were creating handheldgames, but couldn't compete with Game Boy, often because these other systems weren't as convenient to carry around, the color graphics weren't as good, or they went through battery power much too quickly.

In 2004, the Nintendo DS (double screen) was released,

which had two LCD screens. The bottom screen was a touch screen, which allowed a player to lead a game character or navigate menus, and also draw on the screens. Nintendo DS also had the ability to play Game Boy Advance games. Its wireless communication let players to experience **real-time** multiplayer games, and use PictoChat to write and send messages.

Sony's Play Station Portable (PSP) was released worldwide in 2005, and unlike any other handheld system before it, it could play music and videos, as well as games. Like Nintendo DS, it had wireless technology for multiplayer games, and brightly colored graphics. PSP was Sony's first handheld system.

Game Developers and Handheld Game Design

Developing games for a handheld system follows the same process of brainstorming and storyboards as other types of games, but these games have some unique design requirements.

In an article for *Game Biz,* an online magazine for video game designers, a writer wrote about his job designing a game for the Nintendo DS version of Spider-Man 2: "Our focus was on showing off the capabilities of the DS— namely the 3D graphics, dual-screen and touch-screen. Our goal for *Spidey PSP* was to bring a very cinematic feel to the game experience—something the PSP was ideally suited for. That meant a lot of focus on pushing the graphics. . . . New CG [color graphics] sequences were created and the storyline, although loosely based on the movie, had lots of new chapters. The game play was similar to the console games [PS2 and Gamecube] but all the content, level design etc. was brand new—exclusive to the PSP."

Chapter 6

Becoming a Computer Game Designer

WHERE DO COMPUTER GAME DESIGNERS WORK?

MANY VIDEO GAME DESIGNERS work for large game publishers such as Nintendo, THQ, and Activision. But their skills in programming and design are useful in a variety of other fields as well. For example, publishers of educational software need people to design programs for CD-ROM games, to help young students learn to read and write.

Designers can also work in the entertainment industry at large studios, such as Disney, as animators, artists, and texturers. Disney theme parks use designers to create fantasy environments.

Large corporations hire game designers to create training and simulation software for flight instruction for pilots and military defense, and for flight safety. Retailers hire game designers to create enticing interactive displays in their stores or on their Websites.

In the computer game industry, there is an increasing demand for video game programmers who can work on a game engine, modeling software or 2D and textures. Audio artists in the game industry have training in audio engineering, and can work in the film, video, or computer industry, laying down **soundtracks**, or in the advertising or recording industries. Casinos and the arcade industry hire computer game developers to create games for arcades and for online gambling.

SCHOOLS, SKILLS, AND TRAINING

More than 80 colleges, including MIT, the University of Chicago, and Princeton, now offer programs in video and computer game design. Game software is a very competitive field. In fact, worldwide, it is a $28 billion industry, and designers are the people who bring it all together.

The basic technical skills you'll need to become a video game designer begin with math, since computer software and video game systems are based on mathematical **formulas**. A solid background in game systems of all types and computers is also essential.

Programmers must know **calculus** and **linear algebra**, to give them the background they need to create 3D games. **Data structures** training is also important, since it is the digital foundation of modeling software. Programmers must also be skilled in algorithms and computer graphics.

Colleges and Universities
DigiPen Institute of Technology

DigiPen Institute of Technology, located near Seattle, Washington, offers a Bachelor of Science degree program in game development. It claims to be the first school in the world to offer four-year degrees in this field. Students can

Current Jobs in Video Game Development

Animator
Artificial Intelligence Programmer
Artist
C++ Games Developer
Cinematic Coordinator
Creative Director
Director of Galaxies/Video Games
Executive Senior Producer
Exporter Programmer
Games Systems Engineer
Graphics Network Video Game Designer
Junior Video Game Tester
Level Designer—Video Game Programmer
Multimedia Design Engineer
Native Language Game Tester
Producer e-Commerce—Media Entertainment
Senior Game Designer
Software Engineer
Tools/Engine Video Game Programmer
3D Studio Max Engineer C++
Vice President, Interactive Gaming
Video Game Art Director
Video Game Designer
Video Game Programmer
XBOX Console Tools Video Game Programmer

choose either a two-year or four-year program in game design.

At DigiPen, students learn the skills they need to create games and animation, how to work in teams, complete projects, and produce work on a schedule. DigiPen offers four-year degree programs in Real-Time Interactive Simulation, Computer Engineering, and Production Animation. The school also has a two-year program in 3D Computer Animation, along with summer workshops, and outreach programs.

Carnegie Mellon University Entertainment Technology Center

The Entertainment Technology Center (ETC) at Carnegie Mellon University in Pittsburgh, Pennsylvania, is different from other technology arts schools because student learning is project-based rather than course-based. According to ETC's curriculum overview, "[S]tudents devote most of their energy (and do most of their learning) as members of interdisciplinary teams completing projects in lieu of taking traditional classes. In fact our students usually spend 80% of their 'school/work/study' time devoted to projects!" The backbone of the ETC curriculum is a sequence of project courses, each of which places students in **interdisciplinary** teams.

Students rotate through a variety of projects that take different periods of time to complete: For example, in the Building Virtual Worlds course, teams work together for only two weeks, while in other project courses, teams are together for half a semester or an entire semester.

ETC also offers traditional courses, such as a survey on entertainment technology. The curriculum overview states,

"The students must also take a course in improvisational acting, which teaches students how to make their peers look good, how to tell a story on the fly, and how to create an interactive experience in the theater."

MAKING YOUR OWN GAMES

Many leaders in the computer game industry, such as Noland Bushnell and Will Wright (creator of The Sims), got their start in the business by creating their own games and marketing them.

If you want to create your own video game, there are plenty of software programs designed especially for the **amateur**. In addition to design and modeling software, these programs offer tutorials, advice on breaking into the business of game design, and step-by-step processes for how to plan, design, and create game environments and characters.

Another way to get your game published is to get a team of programmers, designers, and artists together who are as excited about your game and the business of game design as you are. Create as much of the game as you can and make a "**demo**" to show publishers that you know what you're doing and that you're serious about the business of computer games.

Chapter 7

Profiles in Computer Game Design

SHIGERU MIYAMOTO

SHIGERU MIYAMOTO IS THE JAPANESE game developer who created Nintendo's Donkey Kong, Mario Brothers, Pikmin, and Legend of Zelda video games. He is widely regarded in his profession, and is considered one of the fathers of the modern computer game. He is also considered the most successful game developer of all time (Figure 7.1).

Miyamoto's games are known for their refined control-mechanics and interactive worlds in which the players are encouraged to discover things for themselves. He is currently the director and general manager of Nintendo Entertainment

Analysis and Development (EAD), the corporate branch of Nintendo of Japan. In 1998, Miyamoto became the first person to be inducted into the Academy of Interactive Arts and Sciences' Hall of Fame.

Miyamoto began his career at Nintendo in 1980, and was given the task of designing one of the company's first coin-operated arcade games. The resulting title, Donkey Kong, was a huge success and the game's lead character, Mario, has become Nintendo's mascot. Miyamoto quickly became Nintendo's star producer and built a large stable of franchises for the company, most of which are still active today, decades after they were first introduced.

Shigeru Miyamoto was born in Sonobe-cho, Kyoto, Japan. As a young boy, he loved to draw, paint pictures, and explore the landscape surrounding his home. In 1970, he enrolled in the Kanazawa Munici College of Industrial Arts and Crafts, and graduated five years later. He would later remark that his studies often took a backseat to doodling. In 1977, armed with a degree in industrial design, Miyamoto got a meeting with Hiroshi Yamauchi—a friend of his father, and the head of Nintendo in Japan. Yamauchi hired Miyamoto as a "staff artist," and assigned him to be an apprentice in the planning department.

In Japan, Miyamoto was considered somewhat unusual. He loved bluegrass music, playing the banjo, and the Beatles. More than anything else, he loved to design toys. One of his first jobs for Nintendo was creating the game Radarscope.

In 1979, the president of Nintendo, Hiroshi Yamauchi, called Miyamoto into his office, and asked if he wanted to design an arcade game. Miyamoto happily accepted the offer.

He began work right away, inventing an elaborate story involving a gorilla escaping from his master, a carpenter called Jumpman. When the gorilla ran off, he also took the carpenter's girlfriend. The gorilla climbed to the top of a seven-story building, and when Jumpman followed, the gorilla fought him off with rolling barrels. The carpenter had to jump over the barrels to stay in the game. When the carpenter reached the top of the building, the gorilla ran to another building, which was even higher. Now the carpenter had to avoid flames as he made his way toward the gorilla and his girlfriend, pulling at and destroying the structure that the gorilla was standing on. When the structure was completely destroyed, the carpenter got his girlfriend back.

Figure 7.1 Shigeru Miyamoto (right) poses with Mario, star of the original Donkey Kong game and the mascot of Nintendo.

The Nintendo game Radarscope was launched in the United States, but failed. In its place, Nintendo wanted an arcade game, and Miyamoto's gorilla and carpenter scenario was introduced in the United States after its initial success in Japan. After consulting with some of the company's engineers, Miyamoto completed his game design, and also wrote the music for the game on a small electronic keyboard. The revised game was called "Donkey Kong."

Donkey Kong was an overnight success. Out of the three characters Miyamoto created for the game—Donkey Kong, Mario (the renamed "Jumpman"), and Pauline (the girl-friend Mario tries to rescue)—Mario has found the most success. Since his debut in Donkey Kong, he has appeared in more than 100 games spanning over a dozen gaming platforms.

WILL WRIGHT

Will Wright was a bookworm who built toy ships and model planes as a child. As a college student, he studied architecture and mechanical engineering at three universities over a period of five years, but he never got his degree. Today, it would appear that his love of learning has paid off, even without the degree, since Wright is considered a genius for his invention of the computer simulation game SimCity. He got the idea for the game while working on a game called Raid on Bungeling Bay, where helicopters attack islands. Wright discovered that he enjoyed creating the islands more than attacking them, and the idea for a simulated city, SimCity, was born.

He created his own version of it for the Commodore 64 system. The game wasn't an instant success, so Wright formed his own company, called Maxis, to promote it. He started the company with another game designer named Jeff Braun, whom he'd met at a pizza party. They created and published versions of SimCity for PCs and Macintosh computers, and handled all tech support from Jeff Braun's apartment.

The "Sims games" are real-time strategy games where players create and furnish an average house while looking after the needs of a virtual family. Unlike the typical video game formula of death and destruction, Sims games are based on daily life in the suburbs. Like real life, if food is cooking on the stove, and someone forgets about it, fires break out, and the fire department comes. If burglars break in, the police are called. You can pick any job you want, as long as it's one of the choices available in the game's Internet or newspaper classified advertisements. Be a movie star, soldier in training, or a pop star—the choice is yours. You get to choose your personality characteristics, astrological sign, hair color, and level of intelligence.

In Sims 2, players direct the Sims as they pass on genetic traits from one generation to the next, witness their life-changing moments from cradle to grave, and make movies about them. Players create the cast, operate the camera, and write the screenplay. The newest versions are SimCity 4, The Urbz—Sims in the City, The Sims Bustin' Out, and The Sims Megadeluxe.

ACTIVISION INTERVIEW

In the following interview, Gregory John, a senior producer at Treyarch/Activision, discussed his work.

> *Are storyboards used throughout the development of a game, or only in the beginning?*
>
> Storyboards are mainly used from the beginning through the middle of the project to design our animated cut scenes.

Are storyboards posted on walls in a meeting room for everyone to discuss?

The storyboard artist, the animators, and the designers of the mission all sit in a room with several large whiteboards and design an animated cut scene. Using a whiteboard makes editing very simple. Once we're done, we take a digital picture of the whiteboards and we post them to our internal Website so everyone on the team can view them.

What are you currently working on?

We're currently in preproduction on a project that has not been revealed yet.

What were some of the brainstorming ideas for the Spider-Man game?

For Spider-Man 2, the most successful ideas we came up with were the realistic web swinging and the gigantic New York City. When we brainstorm, we write down everything without criticizing any ideas. After we get everything logged, we then start sifting through the ideas and following the paths to see if the ideas will lead to interesting game play.

Which modeling software do you use?

We use 3D Studio Max to do all our 3D modeling.

What is the process of giving a character movement and personality?

It starts with character design and then a 3D model. A lot of the personality is established by the model and the texture map (the paint job we give the model). During the character design, we also decide how the character will move. We use traditional 2D concept drawings similar to flipbooks to rough out the movements and guide the animators. The animators, of course, then animate the character.

Is there a difference between a character artist and an animator?

It really just depends on how companies name the positions.

At Treyarch, we have character modelers, character texture artists, and animators (who usually do both character animation and cut scene animation).

Where would you recommend that kids go for training to become video game designers?

I think the best training is playing lots of games—board games, video games, card games. The key is to think deeply about the game experience and mechanic. Mathematics, logic, and statistics are the fundamental tools needed to analyze game play. As a game designer, you must also write and speak well, so that you can articulate your game design ideas.

Do brainstorming sessions occur throughout the development process, or only once, at the beginning?

The majority of the brainstorming occurs at the beginning; however, anytime we run into an area that has been under-designed, we assemble a brainstorming meeting to come up with ideas.

Schools in the United States With Game Development Programs

Academy of Art University

Academy of Game Entertainment Technology

Art Center College of Design

Art Institute of Atlanta

Art Institute of California (Santa Monica)

Art Institute of California (Orange County)

Art Institute of California (San Diego)

Art Institute of California (San Francisco)

Art Institute of Charlotte

Art Institute of Colorado

Art Institute of Dallas

Art Institute of Fort Lauderdale

Art Institute of Las Vegas

Art Institute of Philadelphia

Art Institute of Phoenix

Art Institute of Pittsburgh/Art Institute online

Art Institute of Portland

Art Institute of Seattle

Art Institutes International Minnesota

Bristol Community College

Brooks College

Brown University

California Institute of the Arts

California Polytechnic State University

Cal State Fullerton

Cal State Long Beach (University College & Extension Services)

Carnegie Mellon University Entertainment Technology Center

Center for Digital Imaging Arts at Boston University

Center for Electronic Communication at Florida Altantic University

Cerro Coso College Academy of Digital Animation

Champlain College

Clover Park Technical College

Cogswell Polytechnical College

College for Creative Studies

Collins College

The Community College at Baltimore County

DePaul University's School of CTI

DeVry University

DH Institute of Technology

DigiPen Institute of Technology

Drexel University

Edmonds Community College

Expression College for Digital Arts

Florida Atlantic University

Full Sail Real World Education

Game Institute

Gemini School of Visual Arts and Communication

Georgia Institute of Technology

Georgia State University

Gnomon School of Visual Basics

The Guildhall at Southern Methodist University

Illinois Institute of Art, Chicago

Illinois Institute of Art, Schaumburg

Indiana University—MIME Program

Marist College

Massachusetts Institute of Technology

Mercy College, Center for Digital Arts

Mesmer Animation Labs

Michigan State University

Multimedia and Digital Communications at the Digital Media Institute of Oklahoma

New York University, The Center for Advance Digital Applications

Northwestern University Computer Science Department

Otis College of Art and Design, Digital Media Department

Palomar College

Parsons School of Design

Platt College, San Diego School of Design

Pratt Institute

Purdue University

Ringling School of Art and Design

Rochester Institute of Technology

San Francisco State University/College of Extended Learning (Multimedia Studies)

Savannah College of Art And Design

School of Communication Arts

School of Visual Arts

Seattle Central Community College

3D University

University of Advanced Technology

University of Baltimore

University of California, Irvine

University of California, Los Angeles (Extension) UCLA

University of Maryland, Baltimore County (Computer Certification Training Center)

University of Michigan (EECS Department)

University of Missouri—Columbia (College of Engineering)

University of Southern California, Interactive Media Division, School of Cinema-Television

University of Texas at Dallas, Institute for Interactive Arts & Engineering

University of Washington Educational Outreach

Video Games at the Movies

algorithms: Systematic methods of solving problems.

amateur: A person who does something because he/she enjoys it and not for money or pay.

analog: A system of measurement that corresponds in numbers to the amount of sound, temperature, or electric current being measured.

animatics: A series of drawings that are photographed to resemble a movie.

artificial intelligence: A software application that game designers use. It controls the movement of objects and characters and detects interactions and collisions.

background art: The sky, scenery, or a cityscape.

budget: A plan or schedule for spending money.

bugs: Errors in software that cause a game to function improperly.

bytes: A string of eight bits is a byte; bits and bytes are the units in a numbering system that designers use to create software programs.

C/C++: Software languages game designers use.

calculus: A branch of mathematics.

cinematographers: People who work with the art and science of photography in making films.

concept: An idea or thought.

cut scenes: Short movies that play during a game.

data structures: The digital foundation of modeling software; tools for organizing information in a program.

debugging: Removing software problems in a program.

demo: A short demonstration of a game.

design document: Written plan for a computer game that outlines the story and the basic style the game should have.

digital: Using numbers.

fixed shooters: Gun-like devices attached to a video game that enable the player to "shoot."

formulas: Rules or methods for doing something.

frame: A single storyboard used in designing a game.

interdisciplinary: Involving two or more branches of learning.

interpersonal skills: The ability to relate to people.

Java: A software language.

joystick: A device for controlling the action in a computer game.

LCD: Liquid crystal display; a display that uses liquid crystal "sandwiched" between two glass plates.

lead programmer: The programmer directing a project.

level designers: People responsible for deciding what each level of a game's action will include.

linear algebra: A branch of algebra that deals with linear (relating to lines) equations.

mission: A special task with a significant purpose.

motion capture: A film technique where actors place sensors on their bodies and computers record their movements for use in animation.

oscilloscope: An instrument that shows images on a fluorescent screen.

paint programs: Software programs that simulate paint.

patent: The exclusive right to make, use, or sell a product one has invented.

player-controlled action: When a player controls the action in a brief film.

polygons: Closed figures with three or more sides; the basis for animated characters and background objects in a video game.

portability: The ease with which something is moved from one place to another.

producer: The person in charge of coordinating and financing all activities in the production of a game.

real-time: Game play where players don't wait for the game to process each play.

retailers: Business owners who sell products directly to consumers.

sensors: Devices that detect or record physical data.

silicon microchip: A tiny set of computer components.

skins: Specially designed game levels and models for characters.

software: Programs that run a computer.

soundtrack: The area along one side of a film carrying sound.

storyboards: Frames of artwork that show rough depictions of what takes place in each part of a game.

studios: The workplaces of artists or designers.

texture mapping: The process of placing a bitmap image on a surface during rendering. Texture mapping creates realistic 3D worlds.

theme: The main idea of a story.

3D engine: The main software of a video game. It renders (makes drawings of) objects, and handles collision detection between game objects.

tool chain: A series of processes for programming computer software.

transistors: Electronic devices that control the flow of electricity in a machine.

vacuum tubes: Components used in early televisions and computers.

Kent, Steven. *The Ultimate History of Video Games*. New York: Prima Publishing and Random House, 2001.

Lund, Bill. *Getting Ready for: A Career as a Video Game Designer*. Mankato, MN: Capstone Press, 1998.

Online.onetcenter.org. "Summary Report for Multi-Media Artists and Animators." 27-1014.00.

Websites

www.gamedesign.net

www.gamedev.net

www.gamespy.com

Crosby, Olivia. "Working So Others Can Play." *Occupational Outlook Quarterly*. Summer 2000. Available online at *http://www.findarticles.com/p/articles/mi_m1155/is_2_44/ai_63257098*.

DeMaria, Russell. *High Score!: The Illustrated History of Electronic Games*, 2nd ed. New York: McGraw Hill, 2003.

Jones, George. *Gaming 101: A Contemporary History of PC and Video Games*. Plano, TX: Wordware Publishing, 2005.

Krantz, Mike. "Video Game College Is 'Boot Camp' for Designers." *USA Today*.

Sellers, John. *Arcade Fever: The Fan's Guide to the Golden Age of Video Games*. Philadelphia, PA: Running Press, 2001.

Websites

www.arcade-history.com

www.bnl.gov

www.gamasutra.com

www.gignews.com

www.uat.edu

www.wikipedia.org

ABOUT THE AUTHOR

MARY FIRESTONE grew up in North Dakota. She lives in St. Paul, Minnesota, with her 11-year-old son, Adam, their pet beagle, Charlie, and cat, Rigley. She has a bachelor's degree in music from the University of Colorado at Boulder, and a master's degree in writing from Hamline University. When she isn't writing articles for magazines and newspapers and books for children, she enjoys gardening and spending time with her son.